This book is dedicated to my beautiful wife and amazing daughter.

May your light shine, always.

Wish you enough!

The summer for animals, means fun in the sun.
Some dig trenches, some climb, some soar and some run.

With days this long, so many things can be done.

Bunny hops around until he can't hop anymore.
Whale dives deep, way down to the ocean floor.
Bird spreads her wings and flies until she's
merely a speck.

Hippo lies under water and gets tons of rest. Cow loves to graze and eat as much food as he can, but fun comes much later for the diligent Ant.

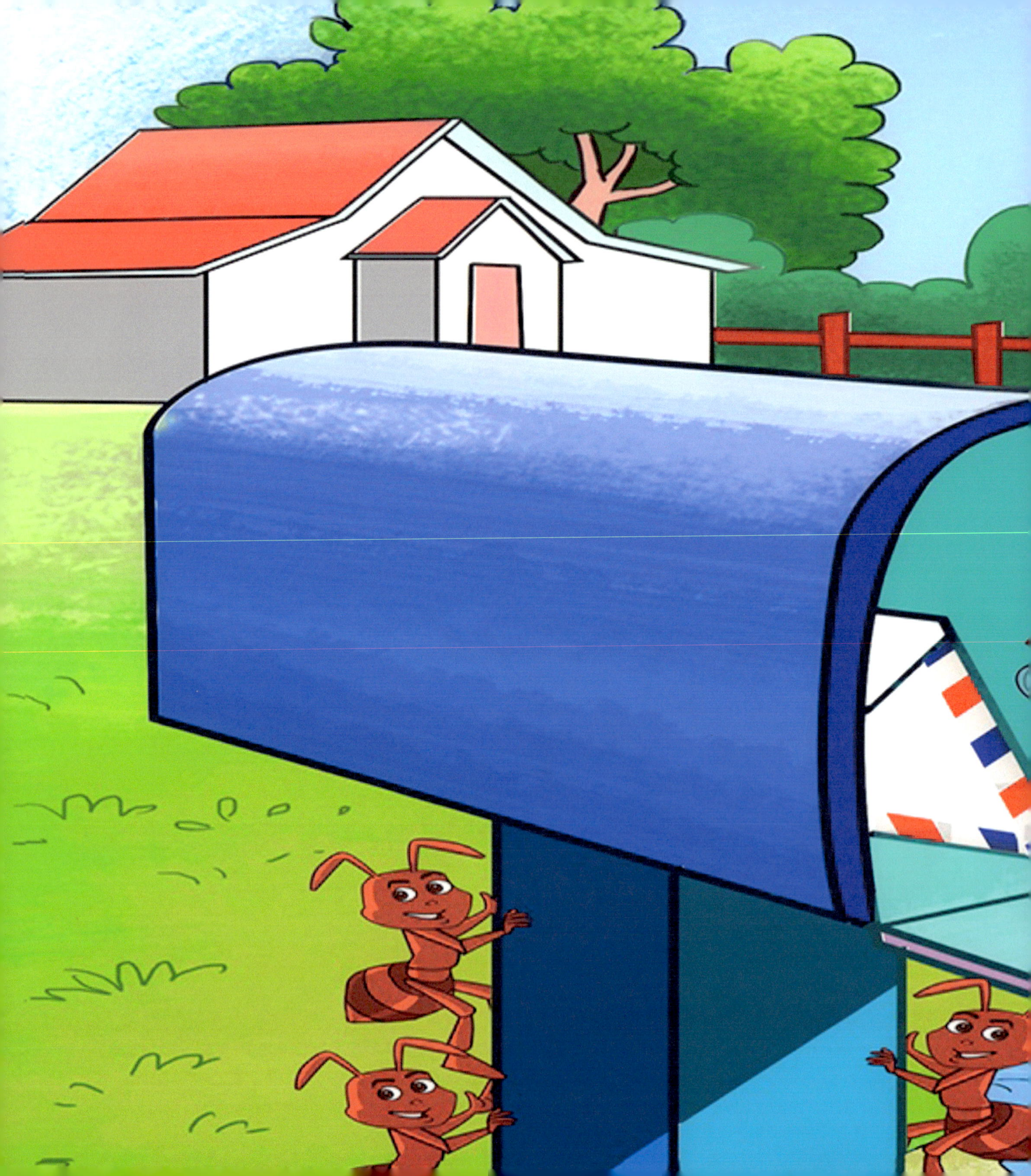

They trek, they hike, they climb and they trail. They scavenge through everything, even your mail. They go out in search of tools, utensils, water and food. They store it up high until it fills every room.

One day as the ants went out,
Cow trots by and says with a shout,
"The sun is out and all you do is work, my friends! Don't you want to mooo-around and eat all that you can?"

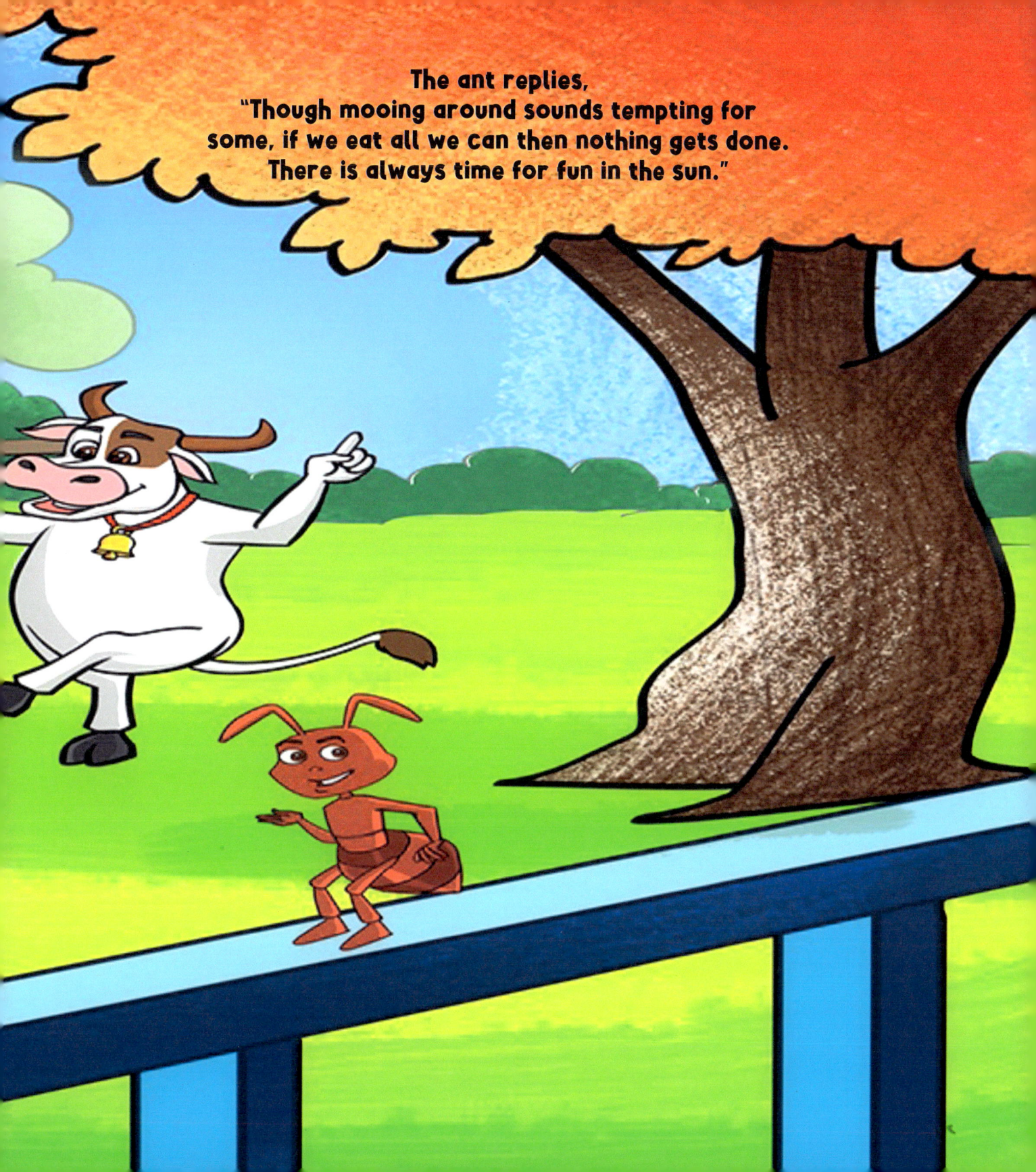

The ant replies,
"Though mooing around sounds tempting for some, if we eat all we can then nothing gets done. There is always time for fun in the sun."

Then Bird said with a screech as she flew by, "Don't you want to fly so high, you become one with the sky?"

"There is always time to fly!"
The ant announced.
"We'll get so high we can flip upside down,
but for now we must get everything under the ground."

Then Whale jumped out of the water and said with an echoing roar, "Don't you want to dive way down deep and explore? There are creatures and treasures and wonders galore."

"Well, Mr. Whale, that does sound like loads of fun. But if we go exploring now, our work won't get done and it's almost impossible when there is no sun."

Bunny whizzed by and just had to proclaim, "Summer's almost over and you haven't yet played! Soon the sun will be gone and there will be snow on the ground. And you wouldn't have danced, or dove, or hopped all around!"

Ant replied, "To hop or to dive or to fly would be fun, but it is hard to survive without food when we can't see the sun."

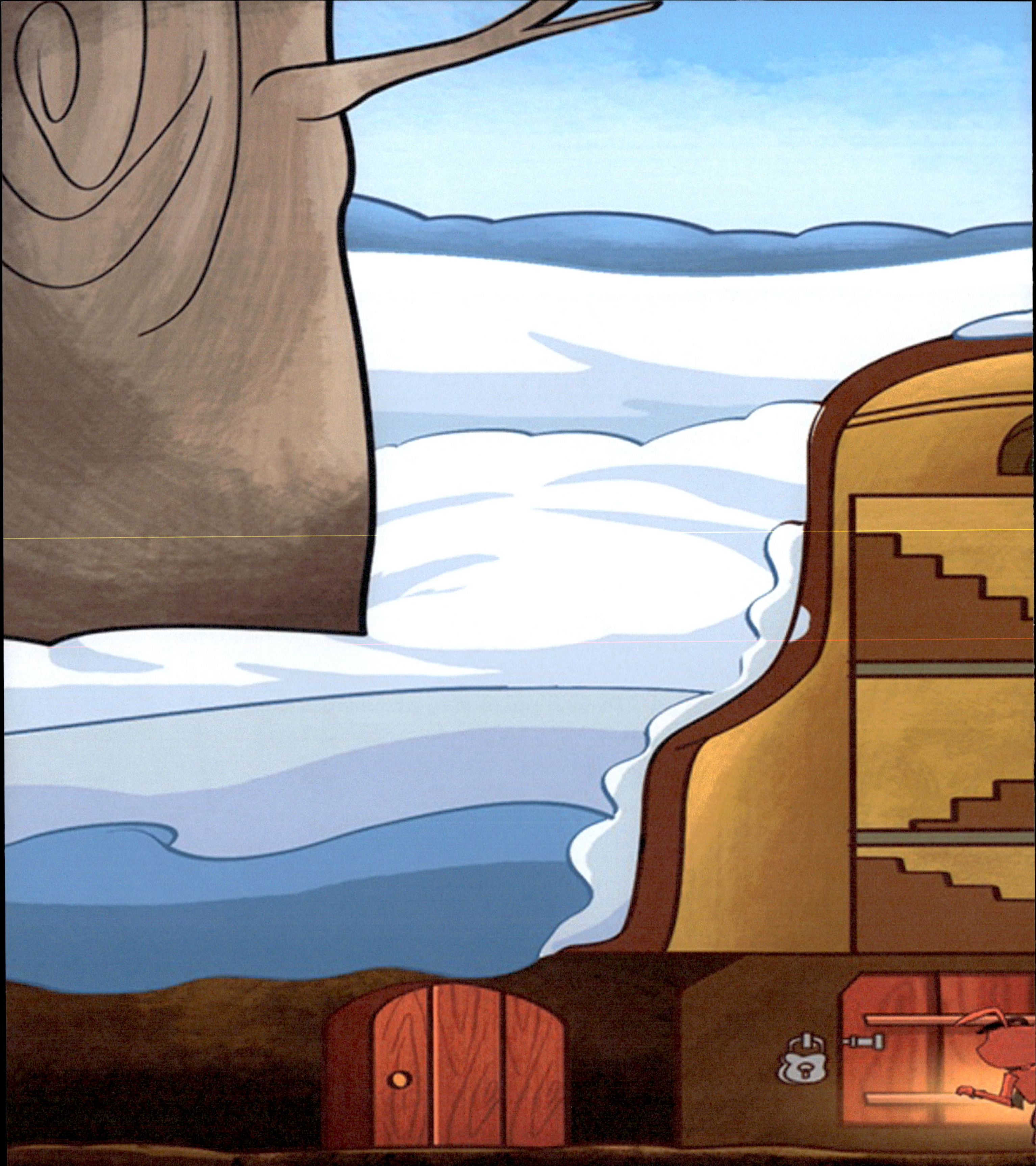

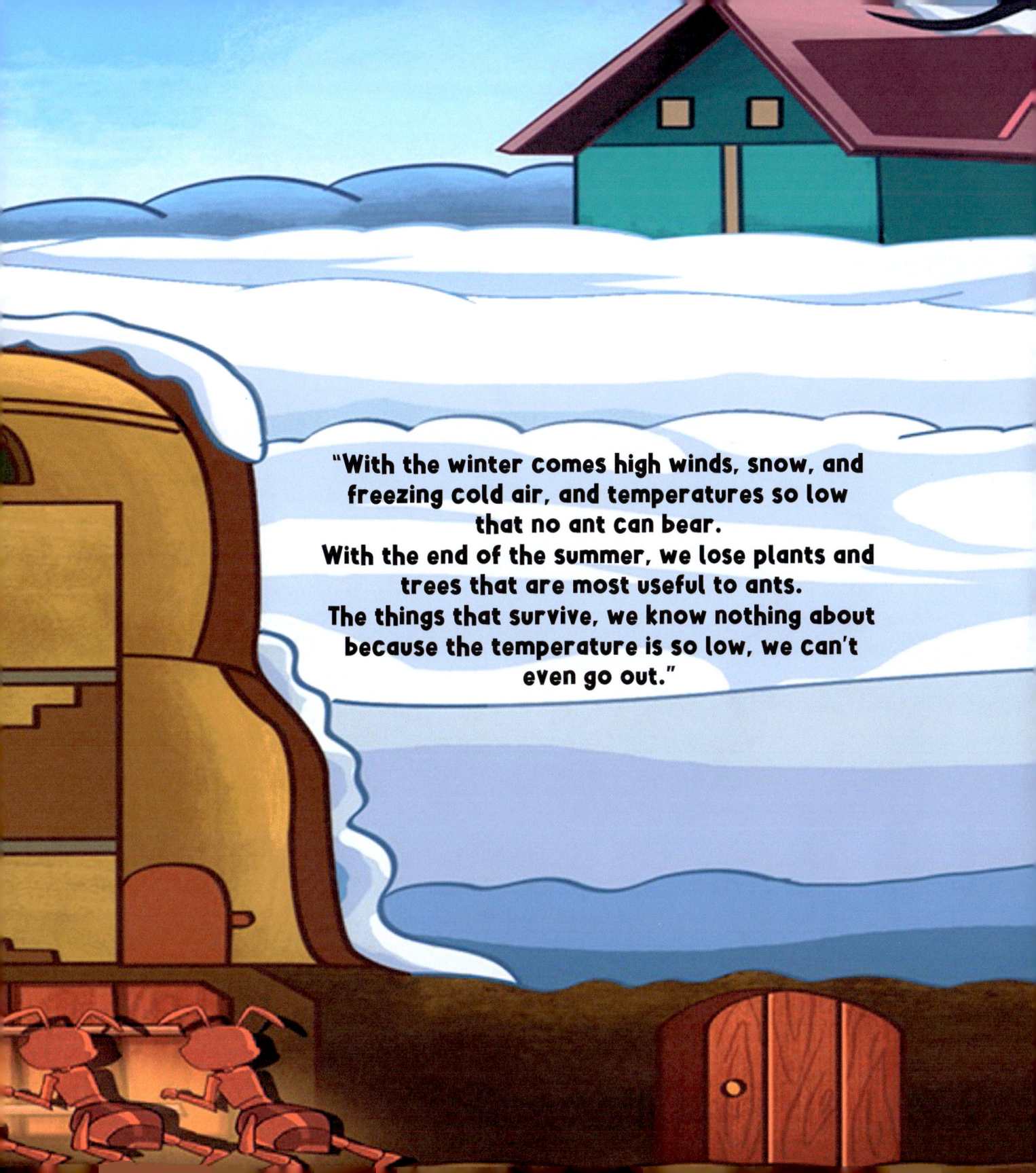

"With the winter comes high winds, snow, and freezing cold air, and temperatures so low that no ant can bear.
With the end of the summer, we lose plants and trees that are most useful to ants.
The things that survive, we know nothing about because the temperature is so low, we can't even go out."

"We take a piece for tomorrow of what we bring in today, so we can have water and food for each winter day. We store and we pack, we collect and we save, but we still know life should not be all work and no play. If you come down here and look real close, we'll redefine fun because we have it the most."

"Yes, we run and we hop, and we fly and we dive, but we also climb and we row, and we—
"Toast?" Bunny interrupted.

"Yes! We toast marshmallows and cookies and fried food in a pan. We double in size from eating all that we can."

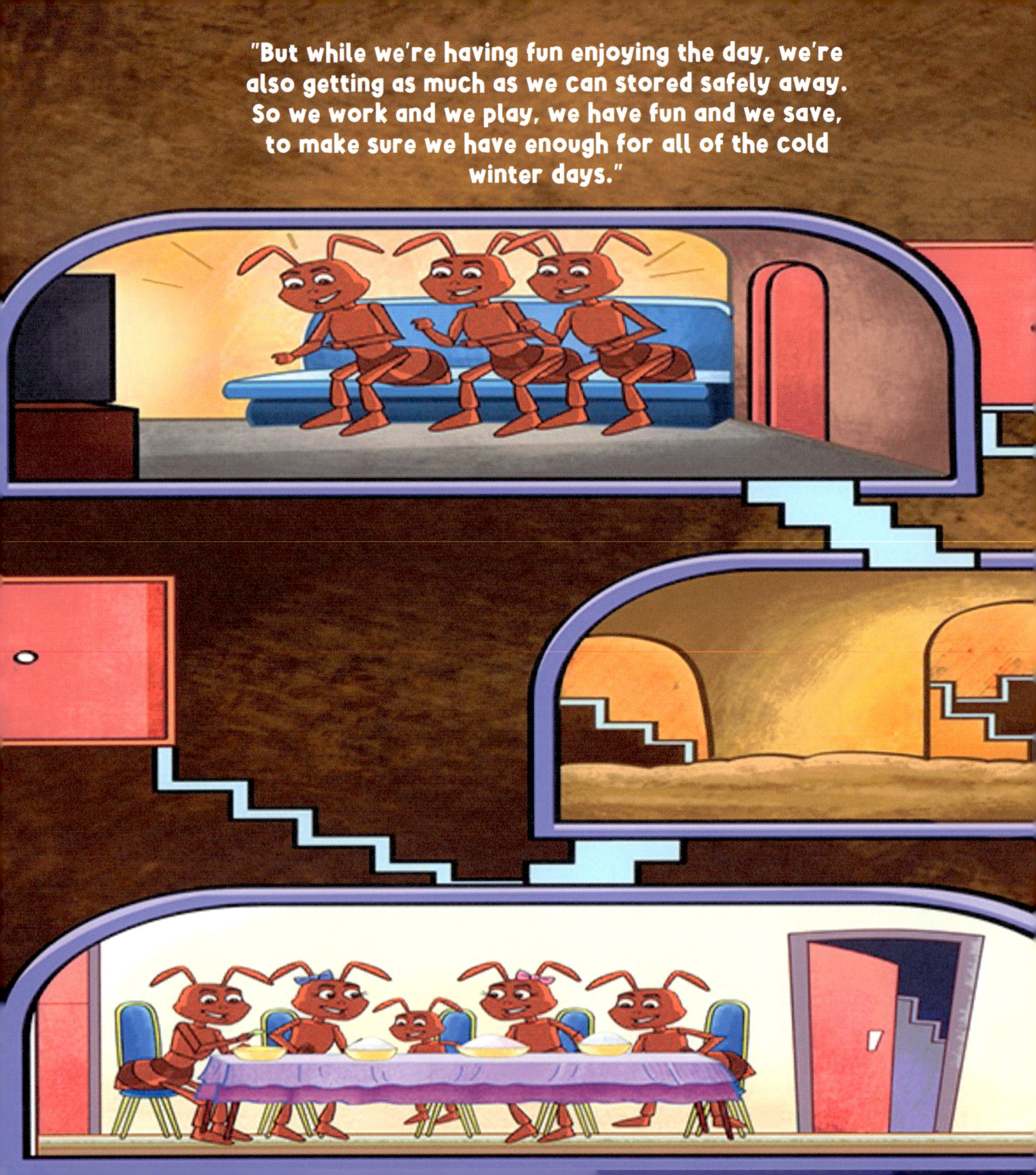

"But while we're having fun enjoying the day, we're also getting as much as we can stored safely away. So we work and we play, we have fun and we save, to make sure we have enough for all of the cold winter days."

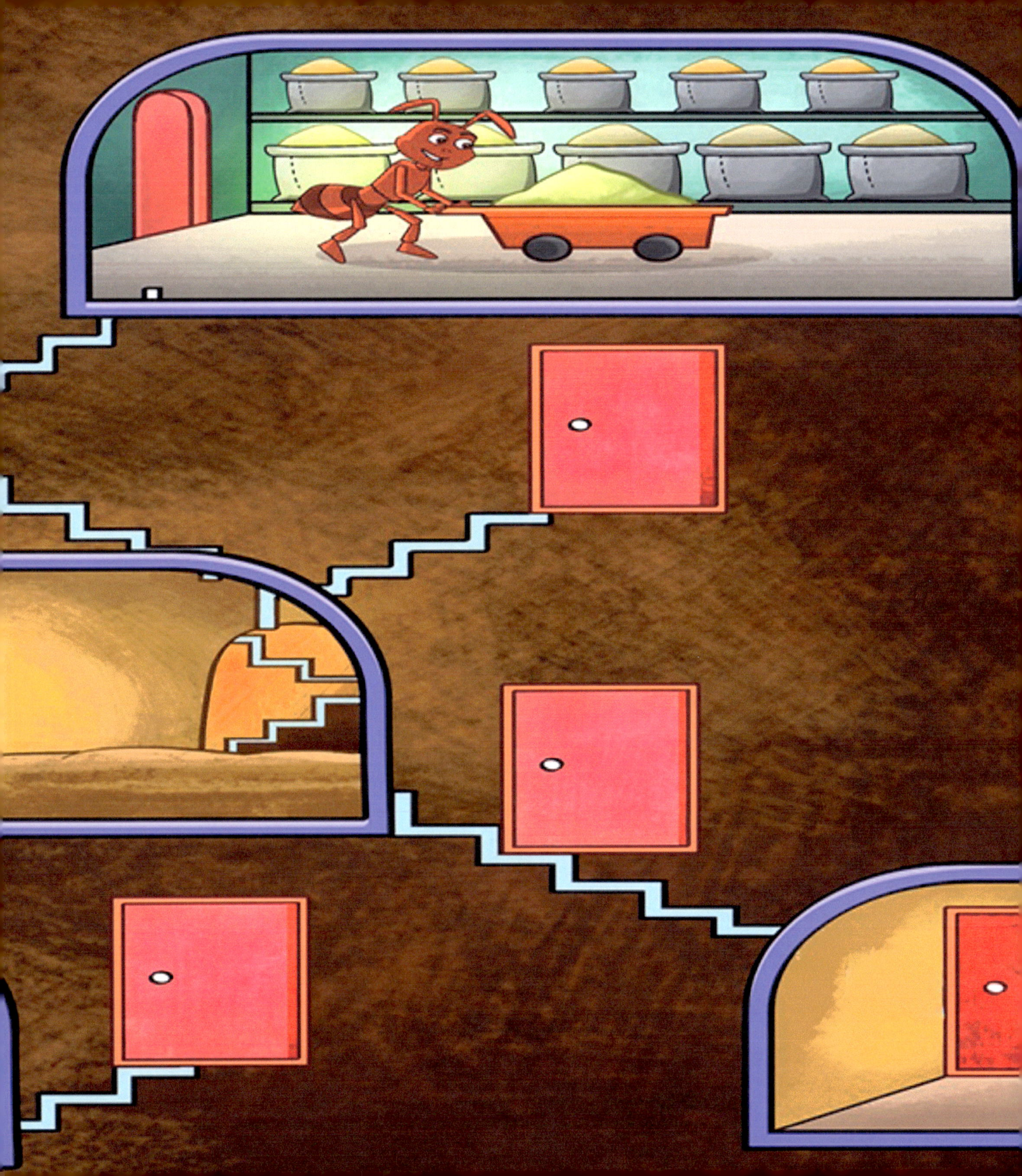

"So we check and we prod to make sure we have the right amount, and if things seem off, we do a recount.

Because if we party too hard, what we gathered will soon come to an end, then we would have to go out and do it all over again."

"In the winter, Bird flies south in search of food and heat while Bunny digs and digs way down deep.

To escape the scorching cold waters, Whale travels to warmer seas and Cow has to moooo-ve around in search of green grass to eat."

"Though you may have fun now out frolicking and enjoying the day, winter for you, is all work and no play.

So we try to find balance in all that we do, because when it comes to life there is one simple truth:

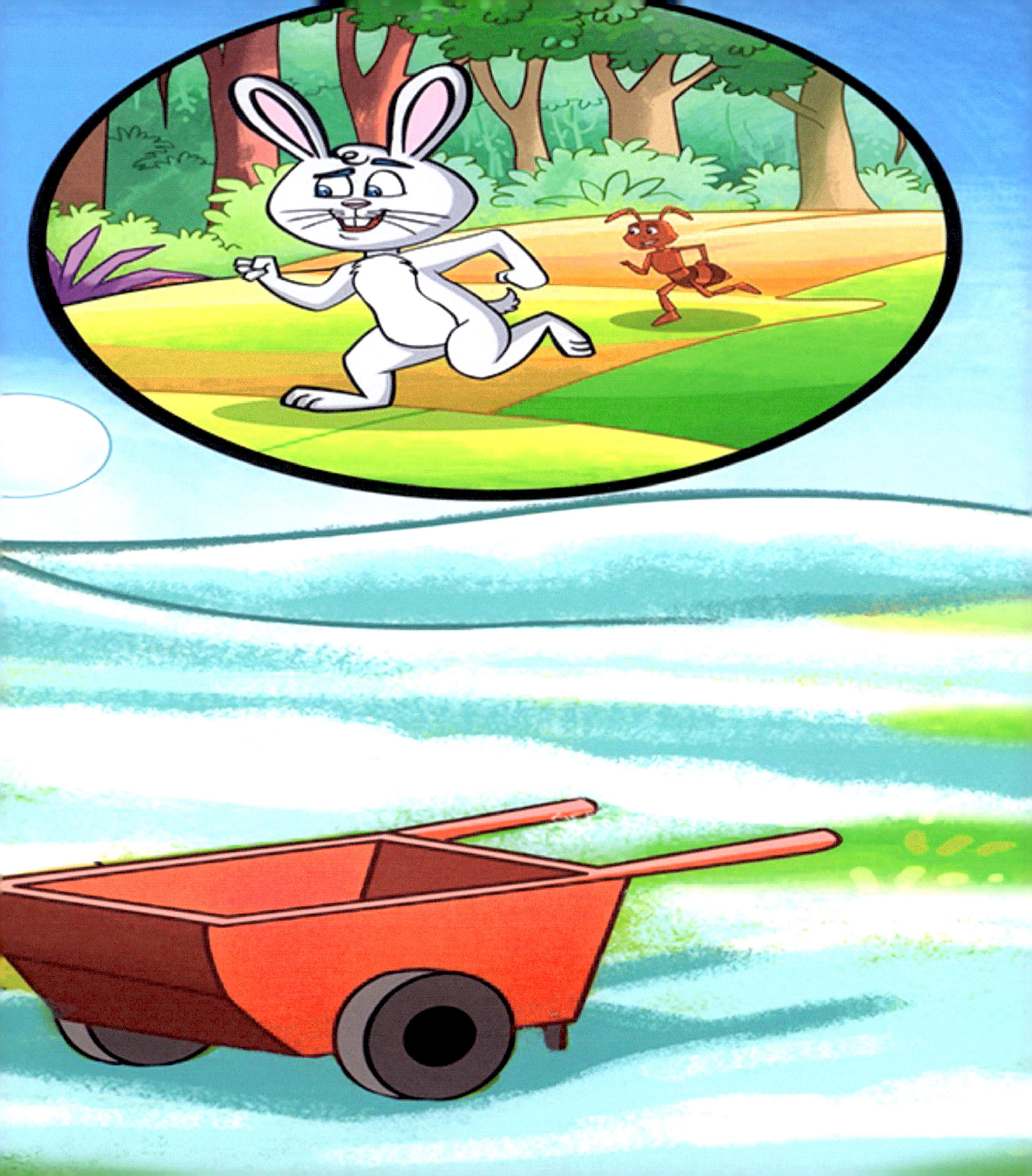

"No matter how fast you run, you hop, or you fly. How much you eat, or how deep you dive, you can never escape work, no matter how hard you try."

WORK
WORK   WORK

"We make the most of the work and save a little each day,

so soon for us it will be less work and more PLAY!"